Lost Trails

and other poems and stories

Willard Hollopeter

ISBN: 978-1-57579-387-0

Library of Congress Control Number: 2008935769

Willard Hollopeter
P.O. Box 686
Wood Lake, NE 69221
402-967-3464
hollopeter@gpcom.net

Printed in the United States of America

PINE HILL PRESS
4000 West 57th Street
Sioux Falls, SD 57106

Acknowledgments

I want to give credit for this book, which seemed like it was never going to happen, to Mary, who has long been gently persuading me to do another book, who checked the manuscript for spelling and grammatical errors, and sometimes pointed out that if I would make just a little change it would read better.

I appreciate Bob Stetter reading and filing the copy of each poem as I e-mailed it to him. For also watching for errors, but mostly for his encouraging spurring to get this book done.

I certainly need to give credit to long time friend Yvonne Hollenbeck for critiquing my work, for setting up blank book pages on my computer and showing me how to enter my material to get it print ready, and for reminding me for years that I needed to do another book.

I envy and admire the seeming ease with which artist, and rancher, David Dorsey draws a story on a sketchpad.

I need to express my thankfulness for having lived the kind of life, and in a setting, that inspires this kind of art form.

Last but not least, I want to thank all the cowboy poets I have met through the years, who have caused me to want to improve my own poetry, and to keep on writing it.

Willard Hollopeter

Two Old-Time Cowboys

My granddad and his brother took homesteads in southern Brown County, Nebraska.

Granddad John and my grandmother, Florence, raised six boys and three girls on the original homestead, not all at the same time though. The older ones were grown and gone when the younger ones came along.

Granddad John and his brother, Josiah, were of a different temperament. Josiah liked to fight and it was said that he was never licked. If a man outfought him, Josiah would take him on, again and again until he won.

Josiah liked his liquor and frequently over imbibed. I suppose that was why he got into so many fights. I imagine they hated to see him come to Brewster, Nebraska, in Blaine County, because he usually got three sheets to the wind and shot the street lights out as he rode out of town. Josiah was an expert marksman. It was said that if he needed to bore a hole in a chunk of metal, he shot one through with a high-powered rifle.

Granddad was of a tamer nature but he would come down hard on us kids when we did something he figured we shouldn't have done.

Life was certainly not easy for those old boys, in that particular time in history. They did whatever they had to do to get by. Money was tight for most country people but they managed to keep their families fed and clothed. That was long before the present welfare state and most of them would have been too proud to take advantage any kind of dole anyway. They would have figured it was a regular sin to take money they didn't earn with their own two hands.

Granddad died nearly sixty years ago, Josiah sometime before that. Some of the trails they forged have long grown dim.

Grandad John (left) and Great Uncle Josiah (right).

Table of Contents

Cowboy Poetry

Cowboy poetry is gaining in popularity, not only in cowboy country but in places where folks aren't certain of what it is all about.

Which could be difficult to understand the reason for, because cowboy poetry flaunts most of the convention of proper writing. Words are often deliberately misspelled and mispronounced. Grammar and punctuation are abused. And cowboy poetry thumbs its nose at political correctness, in fact revels in being politically incorrect.

I think the reason it is so popular is that it is a brave, honest form of art. It chips away the enamel and exposes the raw nerve. It isn't concerned about being flowery or socially acceptable. The good cowboy poetry, written by folks who know what they are writing about, is about unvarnished western life rough side out.

Certainly not all cowboy poetry is about actual happenings, but if the most of the happenings in poems written by real cowboys didn't happen they surely could have.

Cowboy poetry is honest and unpretentious, it is down to earth and about a lifestyle that, though many find attractive or romantic, is one that if they were given a chance to live it they would choose not to do so for long. They would go back to an easier, softer and predictable way of life that they had known before.

Most of those who have not had a working acquaintance with the cowboy way of life couldn't begin to measure up, and that is how it is with writing honest to goodness cowboy poetry.

Some would be writers of cowboy poetry just couldn't begin to measure up in poetic endeavors. The writer has an edge on writing authentic cowboy poetry if he has bucked off a rank horse, or ridden in pelting rain or through snowdrifts in below zero weather. If he has taken his dallies and has had some hairy cowboy wrecks. If he has struggled to save sick calves, has put a horse down who has been like a good friend, and if he has wondered how he was going to get the bills paid.

Only then does the real, honest, believable, down to earth, story telling cowboy poetry emerge. It comes from experience. It comes from the heart.

Introduction

I have ranched in the Nebraska Sandhills most all my life.

There have been good times and there have been hard times. There has been laughter and there has been sadness. Through it all I have gathered up a wealth of material for my poetry.

Along with that ranching experience, I have a pretty good imagination. My poetry has just enough reality to it so that, if it didn't actually happen, it surely could have. I have also found that one essential ingredient to writing poetry is being able to laugh at myself.

I am an avid historian. I enjoy reading accounts from long ago, of the people who settled this country, of the old-time ranchers and cowboys who came up the trail from Texas with their herds of longhorn cattle. Maybe some of that interest stems from the fact that I go back quite a ways myself, not quite that far, but I have lived in a house without electricity, where running water consisted of running it into the house in a bucket from the pump in the yard, and the bathroom facilities were in a little shed back in the yard... way back. In fact, I go back just far enough that I got in on the tail end of picking up cow-chips for stove fuel.

I got my elementary education, up to the ninth grade, in a little one room country school, with none of the modern conveniences. Come to think of it, I am amazed that I actually advanced so far into the modern age as to use a computer.

Some of my poems and stories are about those early days.

Willard Hollopeter

Dedication

I am dedicating this book to the memory of
my grandparents, my parents and all the old-timers
who blazed the trail for me to follow.
A trail that took me to a place that allowed
me space to be away from the suffocating
crush of humanity.

Grandpa John standing by the horse.

Lost Trails

I hear pots and kettles clangin',
and I hear old cookie shout
"Come and get it boys,
or I'm gonna throw it out."

We gather round the fire, sipping coffee
strong, 'bout as hot as it can get.
We take our fill of breakfast,
the best I have ever et.

The kid has wrangled in the remuda,
brought them in on a lope.
The boss steps in the rope corral,
a big loop in his rope.

The first dim light of morning
ain't a helpin' much.
In picking out his chosen mount,
in seeing color, marks and such.

His long twine snags the horse,
out of the others, bunched and turnin'.
He grins and says "Get mounted boys.
Let's move out, daylight's burnin'."

Each man ropes a horse
from his allotted string.
We saddle them and mount,
then the spurs begin to sing.

The chilly mornin's makin' 'em hump,
those ponies ain't wantin' to be rode.
They do some pretty fair buckin',
but nary a cowboy gets throwd.

The boss leads out on the circle,
to gather in cattle that day.
And I figure when I hit my soogan,
I'll sure enough have earned my pay

I was born some too late,
to know if I had what it took.
To fill the boots of those old cowboys,
I read about in a western book.

But I can dream of being in
this picture in my mind.
A scene from out of the past,
Just traveling back in time.

Photo from the Montana Historical Society.

2

Bad Ride

The history of the American west is crowded with stories of good rides and bad horses... or maybe the other way around. Some of them are pretty much the way it happened, and some mostly hot air.

I've got a story that, though the riding wasn't all that good, is sure enough true. I figure a fellow would have a tough time making a story like this one up, no matter how handy he is at spinning windies.

We were giving the calves their pre-weaning shots. My son and grandson came out from town, along with a couple other fellows, to help. We set some corral panels up over in the lake pasture, drove the cows and calves in from the various pastures, worked the calves and then drove them back to their respective pastures. I drove one bunch to the east end of the pasture where the corral was so they would be out of the way. This little deal happened while I was riding back.

I was riding a young horse that was beginning to cow some. He hadn't ever bucked but would take a notion he wanted to once in awhile when I started him into a lope. But I never gave him a chance to find out what it was all about.

Now that horse and I had a lot in common...for a good share of the time neither of us were aware of our surroundings. He was ambling along with me half asleep when he just about stumbled over a saltbox.

He was some surprised, to say the least, and swapped ends mighty fast... way too fast considering my state of semi- consciousness. I lost a stirrup and hooked him somewhere in the vicinity of the flank with a spur. I reckon it made him mad, and I guess he must have figured this was as good a chance as any to find out if he could buck

Danged if he didn't do a pretty fair job of it. For maybe four or five seconds, while I was trying to gather up my reins and find some leather to get hold of, I was thinking I had a chance of getting him rode. Then I lost the other stirrup and that was all she wrote.

That colt was bad scared when he figured out what he had done and took off running in the general direction of home. Now I'd had a coiled rope on the saddle and, in the melee, he'd bucked the rope strap off the horn. I got up and was headed for the corral afoot when my dog came trotting past, dragging the rope with the loop around his neck.

Despite the burr in my pride for getting bucked off, I was feeling plumb grateful I hadn't lost my rope. Then I got to thinking, "if that dog was close enough for that loop to fall over his head, he just might have contributed some to the fracas."

Confabulation

Now there's some fellers,
they just ain't much for walkin',
for spit and polish, and socializin',
and they're some sparin' with the talkin'.

Some are short on thinkin',
and it's a true fact, but sad.
Some are mighty poor at relatin'
happenin's, be they good or bad.

And you know the tellin',
it takes a particular kind of tact,
of verbal articulatin', communication,
which some fellers lack.

Mr. Ned had been gone awhile,
been a week away from the phone.
He gave his hired man a call
to check on things while he'd been gone.

"Every thing here's just fine,
finished fencing on the north side.
Don't worry about a thing,
have fun... Oh hey, your dog died."

"My dog died, how'd he die,
what happened to old Skeet?"
"Don't know, just died,
maybe ate too much burnt horse meat."

"I tried to get them out,
but back they kept turnin'.
You know how horses won't leave
a barn that is burnin'."

"Oh no, my big new barn gone,
and all my horses too.
How'd it happen, why'd you let it,
WHERE WERE YOU?"

"Well – while I was away,
at the funeral for your spouse.
The barn... it caught a spark,
from the ashes of the house."

Granddad kept a bottle hid out so grandma wouldn't know he had
it. Dad and his brother found it and, from time to time, would take a
drink from it, carefully noting the liquor level and replacing what they
drank with water.

Time came when granddads' liquor got so weak he figured out
what was happening. As punishment he tied their hands together
around a tree, with the intention of alternately whipping each one.
Dad, being the stronger of the two, kept his brother on the whip side.

Wouldn't there be a great gnashing of teeth of folks who don't be-
lieve in punishing a child, if they were to read this? They did both turn
out all right though.

All the years I ranched I wouldn't have cast much more of a shadow than a fence post. Then I quit ranching and started gaining weight. Thankfully I have slimmed down some. I wrote this, out of frustration, at that time.

Over the Belt Cowboy

He rode with ease, supple as you please,
thin and lithe and proud.
Tough to the bone he rode alone,
now he himself makes a crowd.

The horses are taller, and he tends to waller
when he's getting mounted up to go.
And he wants his horses tame. He don't aim
on ridin' in no rodeo.

For proper attire young cowboys aspire
to a big buckle, and they tuck in their shirts.
They are keen for that buckle to be seen,
but on him... the buckle just hurts.

The edge is thin, and it 'bout cuts in
to the belly that reposes thereon.
He tries pulling it in, he'd like to look thin,
but the pulling in muscles are gone.

He wants to be fit. If he could just be a bit
of a semblance of that strong young man.
He tries working out, but his body does shout
in protest to his exercisin' plan.

A hat he'd proudly wear on wavy thick hair,
now pride has turned to functional instead.
To keep the hot sun from baking like a bun,
...the top of his pale bald head.

The Wreck

I was sortin' cows the other day,
when a bunch quittin' critter
decided to go her own way.
She was snortin' and slobberin'
in her quest to be free,
the far distant hill was all she could see.
The gleam in her eye showed,
she'd like to eat a cowboy like me.

She headed up a draw, flat movin' out,
in her one track mind, escapin' no doubt.
I tickled Joe's ribs, his attention I won,
and we took out after the sun of a gun.
We overhauled her fast; "Cow we're gonna teach you,
we're gonna show you what a good horse can do.
You're gonna know what a cow horse is for,"
and we turned her like the latch on an outhouse door.

We turned that ornery bunch quittin' beast,
trouble was, Joe headed west, and I was still goin' east.
I grabbed for the horn, but the horn wasn't there,
all I got a hold of, was a fist full of air.
Virgin prairie sod broke my fall,
I bounced kinda like a deflated rubber ball.

When I started breathin' again, I slowly arose,
I wiggled each finger, and wiggled my toes,
then reluctantly, gingerly checked out my nose.
I waved my arms, wiggled my ears and twisted my neck.
To my amazement, discovered I had survived the wreck.

I headed for my horse, thinkin'
I had come out smellin' like a rose.
Slipped in a cow pie and messed up my clothes,
busted my arm and skinned my nose.

There are some good cow dogs. They help a lot in handling cattle.
I would venture to say though, that for every good dog there are a half
dozen who cause more trouble than they help.

Cow Dogs

Most every ranch has a cow dog,
some are smart, some are not.
What these dogs do the best,
is they like a bug critters, a lot.

The way that they chouse a critter
can't be a whole lot refined.
They slip up and nip it on the heel,
and they do it from behind.

It seems, to my way of thinkin'
as a common sense rule of thumb.
If you're gonna bite a critter's heels,
you gotta be might gutsy... or dumb.

Those opinions don't seem to enter
at all into a cow dog's equation.
That's what he's born to do...
It's how we gets his stimulation.

I was startin' a three year old colt,
was gonna give him his first ride.
Had saddled him up, sacked him out,
the dog was layin' off to the side.

I cheeked him, climbed aboard,
but the colt, he just sullied up.
I screwed down, took a bronc rider stance.
That was when the rat-eared speckled pup

decided we needed some more action,
there in the round corral.
In his thinkin' the way to get it,
was the only way he knew so well.

Now cow dogs are bred to heel cattle,
...but a horse will do in a pinch.
Colt took exception to dog's attention,
I had my spurs stuck in the cinch.

I was makin' a terrible sloppy ride.
No bronc rider style there at all.
I grabbed for leather, lost a stirrup,
was dang sure headed for a fall.

He bucked me off, run over me,
with that dog in hot pursuit.
For a plot in a horror movie,
it would have surely been a beaut.

But what irritated me the most,
was that dog was havin' so much fun.
He wasn't just about to quit,
he was getting that horse to run.

Cow dogs love to chase critters,
just about any kind will do.
One thing you need to watch out for,
is they don't chase them over you.

My dad told about when he and mom were newly married, living down a valley not far from another couple. This husband and wife fought a lot and dad said, "if he came out of the house in the morning and heard the neighbor's dog yelping, he knew they had had a fight and he didn't dare try to whip his wife so he whipped the dog."

A Song for Billy

We bedded them there on the Arkansas,
in '76 on a warm Christmas Eve.
Sure hoping they would sleep all night
but then we just couldn't believe

those steers wouldn't take to running,
like they'd done most every night.
They sure enough had it bred in them,
to spook themselves into flight,

And lead us on a wild chase,
in the dark, on a hard run, through
brush, coulees and prairie dog holes.
I tell you, it wasn't no fun.

Me'n Billy was ridin' night guard,
we'd stop and talk as we rode aroun'.
The starless night was black as coal,
those steers was settling down.

He talked about his family back in Texas,
and a sweet girl with flame-red hair.
And how Christmas is a lonely time,
when he knows he can't be there.

He told of his mother singing hymns,
he'd join in on each Christmas day.
He'd sing some parts he could remember,
he was still awhile, then he'd say,

I'm goin' back when the drive is done,
back to that childhood home.
I'm gonna settle in real tight,
and I'm never more gonna roam.

I'm gonna court that red-headed gal,
sweet talk her into bein' my wife.
Gonna raise some corn and kids,
and give up on the ramblin' life.

The cattle started running at midnight,
God only knew the reason why.
We had to get ahead of the herd,
turn those steers. We had to try.

It was too dark to see Billy's horse go down,
in amongst the milling bunch.
But before the cattle got settled down,
I had a terrible sick feeling hunch,

that Billy wasn't going to hear his mother
sing hymns on Christmas day no more.
He wouldn't hold that redheaded girl,
He'd passed on over to Jordan's shore.

We buried him there at daybreak,
in a shallow grave on the cold prairie.
When it come to praying, we wouldn't
know what to say, but I knew that he

liked those hymns his mother sang,
it'd be a fitting way to let him go.
"If you boys would sing a song for Billy,
least ways the words you know."

"Amazing Grace, how sweet the sound,
That saved a wretch like me."

Passing the Torch

"So you young whippersnappers think you're tough"
he said, then he spat in the hoof stirred dust.
"You figure y'all are real good cowboys, doncha?
Hell-fire ranchan hands," he said. "Just

because you can ride and rope some you
think you're as good as they come, but hey.
You kids couldn't have held a candle
to the salty hands back in my day.

And the horses we rode had some bottom,
not like the horses you ride now.
Those horses had to cover some ground,
and those horses knew how to cow.

We didn't haul our horses around,
God made horses to haul us instead.
Many's the time I been ridin' back from a drive,
long after you kids woulda been tucked in bed."

He's not cantankerous or querulous by nature,
but it nags him these young guys don't know or care.
When it come to cowboying with the best,
this old man had damned sure been there.

He does his riding now on the front porch rocker,
dreaming of youth and his time on the range.
Just thinking and wondering, and trying to understand,
why everything he knew had to change.

He thinks of the hard riding he had done,
all of it, he did for not much pay.
Arthritic pain, lonesome and memories,
is about all he'd accumulated that way.

He hadn't had much time for women,
not many women would of took to his way of life.
He'd been over a lot of ground in his time,
wasn't no fitting way for a wife.

He recalls the wrecks that took some friends,
he'd rode with down through the years.
Slim took the trip back in fifty-six,
tied on to a big, stagy roan steer.

Tom hung up in his riggin',
in the arena at Cheyenne.
"A man should be doing what he likes,
when it comes his time for dyin'."

He's been alone now for quite a spell,
he don't know if he's still got family.
And right now this old cowboy is feeling
about as lonesome as a fellow can be.

He gazes out across the hills,
his eyes get sort of misty for awhile.
He takes a deep breath, shoves back his hat,
and then he begins to smile.

"You kids ain't near the hands,
I rode with back in my day.
But it's plain to see you're wantin' to be,
and you're tryin' to do it the cowboy way."

Every once in awhile another old rodeo cowboy rides over the horizon. One by one they are steadily hanging up their spurs and traveling on. Orville Gallino, Dean Kinney, Stan Barent, Elver Lord, Wayne Cornish, Bill Mulligan, Dale and Dess Daniels, Freddy Johnston and Howard Parker, and others I don't recall. My brother Jack could be included in that group. He would have been younger then those he rodeoed with and he left before most of them. It has been twenty- two years since his passing.

All good cowboys, some rode rough stock, others worked the timed events, and some did both. In my limited association with rough stock I didn't achieve, or deserve, near the status as a rodeo cowboy as they did, but I had, and have, great respect for their ability, and the legacy they left.

The Last Rodeo

He carefully measures the hack rein,
to get it just the right length.
A successful ride depends on experience,
more than it does on strength.

He knows this will be his last ride,
he's figuring on going out in style.
But he knows it's time to quit,
he's been knowing it for awhile.

He'd had his share of wins,
but age is a creeping foe.
It robs a man of his ability,
and he knows it's time to go.

One by one, they leave the arena,
their skill remembered by a few.
With respect for what they were,
admiration for what they could do.

May they still throw a fast loop,
and be making a good ride.
Where they'll never be too old,
out there, beyond the great divide.

Dad and Jim.

Dad's Horse, Jim

He was dark sorrel, his most predominate feature was a white rump, the white starting just above the tail head and going down his hind legs. Standing maybe fifteen hands, he had no papers testifying to purity of breeding. He had never ran a race or scored a calf out of a roping chute, but he had dragged many to the branding fire.

The unsung hero and mainstay of cattle country is the ranch horse. I suppose it would be possible to operate a ranch without horses. I hear some do, I don't know how. Maybe those four-wheelers can really replace the horse. I don't think so, I can't imagine sorting cattle out of the herd with one.

Jim was a two year old in 1945 when dad bought and broke him. He remained a stud for two or three years after that, and he was ornery. I think he would have run a mare to death if he had been left with her.

We tend to take a good ranch horse for granted. He is usually around when needed. He is well fed but doesn't get a lot of currying or petting and he likes it that way.

Jim had some bad habits that most horsemen nowadays wouldn't tolerate. But he was gentle. You could pile as many kids on him as would fit and he would take care of them. He was easy riding and he was a cow horse. He knew what a critter was going to do before it did.

When it comes to show most horses couldn't hold a candle to the highly bred, well trained, specialized cutting horse. But the ranch horse has to cut cattle out of the herd and he has to put them somewhere, he usually gets the job done. He has to be a rope horse, a gate closer, sometimes a "Dude" horse, for visiting relatives, and occasionally carry a calf, or whatever he is required to carry. That would blow the minds of most cutting horses

One time my dad, my brother and I were driving cattle. Mom came by in the car and dad was getting tired so he wrapped the reins on the saddle horn and got in the car and went home. Jim continued driving cattle, going back and forth to move the stragglers up.

In the horse world, as with people, are those individuals who, at every opportunity, do less work than is expected of them. But most are honest, giving a hundred percent of all that is asked of them. I once had a little sorrel mare who, I sincerely believe, would have willingly ran herself to death if she had been required to do so.

Dad and Jim liked to clown a bit. When dad broke him, he trained him so he would lay down and play dead, whereupon dad would sit on him and leisurely have a smoke. Standing on the saddle, dad would spin a lariat out full length. I once saw him sitting on a kitchen chair, on Jim's back, rolling a cigarette.

Jim was still going strong when dad died in 1968. He was retired, with the exception of giving a ride to an occasional child. Mom insisted that he die on the ranch so he was leisurely living out the time he had left.

Jim must have been twenty-eight or nine the warm spring evening he came into the corral, wanting to be let in the barn. I was pretty sure he was going to die and I wanted to let him in, but figured I would have a problem getting him back out. With tears in my eyes, I petted him and said goodbye. When I checked on him later he was standing, with hanging head, by the yard gate. In the morning he was laying by the gate.

My first task that morning was to dig a grave. I wasn't about to dump old Jim in a blowout.

Jim

He wasn't much for looks,
and you'd seldom notice him,
if it wasn't for his color.
Dad called him Jim.

With a white rump and rear legs,
he was noticeable for sure.
No papered pedigree was his,
his breeding was far from pure.

Dad bought him as a colt,
and broke him when he was two.
Jim became a top horse...
there wasn't much he couldn't do.

Dragging calves to the branding fire,
or sorting cattle... he took it in stride.
As he did giving city folks,
and their kids, a gentle ride.

He could turn on a dime, leave some change,
and when it come to cutting a cow.
He would beat her at every jump,
he sure enough knew how.

Jim was getting up in age
when dad took his last ride.
It was years later, I shed some tears
the night old Jim lay down and died.

I've known some horses, good and bad,
like good friends, I remember some.
Jim is one that sticks in my mind...
That old pony was as good as they come.

Dad and Jim.

The Pioneers

The story of the pioneers,
and what they went through,
has often been told.
So, what I say here is nothing new.

But I don't believe the story
can too often be told,
of those courageous people,
in the days of old.

They settled the land
when it was wild and new.
Settled it with hardship,
and many sacrifices too.

With the coming of the railroad,
they were encouraged to come and stay.
The railroad needed population,
people to use it, to make it pay.

The passage of the homestead act,
and the free land it did mean.
Brought them by the thousands,
with their families and a dream.

From all walks of life,
and nationalities, they came.
For a chance to make a better life
on their homestead claim.

They lived a hard life,
luxuries, they did lack.
In a dug-out, or sod shanty
or a tarpaper shack.

Their goals were simply to survive,
and to make a home.
And to prove up on the land,
so it would be their own.

They toiled to make it work.
Often they toiled in vain,
against grass hoppers, heat and cold,
and usually not enough rain.

Many couldn't take the life,
some even lost their mind.
Some gave up and went back,
to what they had left behind.

And they sold out to those who
with their claims and dreams did stay.
That was the beginning
of the big ranches today.

The Sandhills ranching families,
 who live the good life today.
Can thank an early relative,
who on his claim did stay.

We wouldn't want to live the way
our forefathers had to.
But we can be thankful
they did what they had to do.

Spirits

There's spirits roaming these hills and, if you haven't gotten sedentary from the comfort of change, if your hearing hasn't become permanently impaired by the roar of diesel engines, and if you can dare to loosen the reins on your imagination, you too can see them and hear them.

Listen carefully. Can't you hear the yelling of cowboys and the bawling of cattle being forced into railroad pens at Wood Lake? Can you hear the commotion and laughter as a drunken cowboy spurs his horse into Swett's barbershop? Can you hear weary sighs and the creak of saddle leather as the drovers dismount in midnight darkness at the home corral?

On the bank of the Calamus, in the meager light of their campfire, I see my granddad and great-uncle sitting on a wagon tongue. I hear them talk of the land they had traveled through that day and I detect concern in their voices as they wonder if the land they chose to claim will be all they had hoped it would be. In the brightness of mid-morning I watch my granddad tightly grip that wagon tongue as his brother stitches a torn lip with darning needle and black patching thread.

I notice the lines around grandma's eyes that tell of the weary struggle of rearing nine children and I see her work-roughened hands clasped in prayer. Praying, no doubt, that I would escape the many evil snares of a modern society she couldn't understand.

My dad is talking quietly to a wild-eyed colt he is preparing to mount. I hear him encourage a four-horse team to pull a load of hay a little further up the hillside to give cattle just a bit more shelter from the blizzards of '49, and I can see him and old Jim dragging calves to the branding fire.

I see dad anxiously peer through the increasing snow for mom's return on the day she rode to her school because the snow was too deep for wheeled vehicles, and I feel the sting of dad's razor strap when I was foolishly disrespectful to he or mom.

Waiting at the corral gate, Old Jim softly tells me he wants his feed. Tim is there, and Sis, and Cactus, and Sam. Tony, no doubt the fastest pony that any kid ever rode, and a pretty good little cow-horse, is waiting, and old Spot.

I hear the applause of the crowd as my brother loosens the wraps, dismounts and gets away from an angry bull. Steer wrestling for Jack is a fine art, and I watch him pick up a double hocker in good enough time to win a go in team roping. He and I have a good natured contest as to who can rope the most calves needing doctoring and we maybe head and heel a cow or two we really don't need to.

Yes, there's spirits roaming these hills. They are watching and trying to understand. I imagine unfamiliar ways make them uneasy so it's up to us to hold onto enough of the old so they can be comfortable.

Old Rake

Just a picture of an old dump rake,
sitting long on meadow ground.
A rusty worn out old horse rake,
with tall grass grown all around.

Slow but sure, it did the job,
making windrows thick and straight.
Technology and wanting to hurry up,
it was that what sealed its fate.

The family's kids likely rode that rake,
though it seemed to take forever.
Before they each got quite big enough,
so their foot could reach the lever.

No one knows the story of that rake,
and how it came to be left there.
Perhaps they also discarded dreams,
and left the place in despair.

As I think back along the years,
back to when that rake was used.
My thinking brings some sadness,
of how our way has been abused

by corporations and politicians,
corroded and corrupted by greed.
If anything could bring a change,
I figure there's a bunch of folks need

to maybe experience just a bit,
of how it was in those days.
Just maybe they would get to thinking
they'd do well to change their ways.

A lot of good old country values
lie idle there with that rake.
Like sealing a deal with nothing more,
than the spoken word, and a handshake

In the 1980s ranchers were having a tough time making it. Some were being sold out. That was the inspiration for this poem.

When it's Shippin' Time Next fall

Though you treat it as a joke,
and laugh about being broke,
(it's been close to true for awhile.)
You worry and you fret
as the expenses, and your debt,
and gol-durned interest begins to pile.
You're sure not getting stronger,
and the tunnel's getting longer,
and you can't see no light at all.
But you've been there in the past,
and you're hoping you can last,
until it's shippin' time next fall.

You know you should have been saving,
you're skimping and you're shaving
on expenses all you can to make do.
Though you've not been one to shirk,
when you've had to do some work,
you don't know as it will work for you.
There shouldn't be this bind
wrecking a man's peace of mind,
no sir, it shouldn't be this way at all.
And for all your hanging tough,
there's just not going to be enough
to go around at shippin' time next fall.

You've got a pretty good banker,
but you surely don't hanker
to have that banker own your place.
Reckon it would make you smile

if you didn't see him for awhile,
that would put a smile on your face.
But you've got yourself a hunch
the market is going to slip a bunch,
it's enough to make a grown man bawl.
And the grass it's going fast,
but you've got to make it last,
until it's shippin' time next fall.

You have taken' to looking back,
down along the bumpy track,
that life has hauled you on this far.
Maybe you wouldn't have this load,
if you had took another road,
to somewhere other than where you are.
But this trail you've traveled down
so far you can't turn around,
right or wrong you've made your call.
It's been rough, an uphill climb,
...this could be the last time,
you'll be shippin' cattle in the fall.

They say all a man needs is a good horse, a good dog, and a good woman. Two out of three ain't bad.

This here story is pretty much true. The mare played a big roll in me figuring out that I might not have been all that much of a bronc rider.
She ended up in a rodeo contractor's bucking string.

Education

Reckon I should have tried breakin' her sooner,
'cause she'd been four summers on Sandhill grass.
Getting the age where she'd be hard to break,
but I figured I might as well give it a pass

at tryin' to make a decent using horse
out of that wild, green, four year old mare.
I was young then, and full of vinegar,
was willing to try ridin' anything with hair.

I sacked her, saddled her, and mounted up.
She stood just like a well broke horse.
Very soon I was sadly to find out,
that was a well thought up resource,

for giving me a false sense of security.
I wasn't at all on no hurricane deck.
She was calm, and still and serene,
and I was starting to think "What the heck,

it ain't gonna take nothin' to break this mare,
why I figured she would throw a fit."
I pulled her 'round and nudged her some,
and that is when the... there was a lot of it

hit the proverbial fan, so to speak.
She swapped ends and broke in two,
she kicked, squealed, made some moves,
of which I had no idea she knew.

It wasn't very long that I rode her,
not very long that I stayed on top.
I was soon layin' in the dirt of the corral,
hearin' those stirrup leathers pop.

Well, I tried her twice more after that,
each time she bounced me like a ball.
Each time I was gettin' more convinced,
I just wasn't no bronc rider at all.

I finally had to face the facts
though it bruised my manly pride...
That mare was learnin' how to buck,
faster than I was learnin' how to ride.

I wish I had long ago known about the relatively new way of break-ing colts, doing a big share of the breaking on the ground, before you ever mount up. It would have surely saved me a bunch of aches and bruises.

In later years I did some groundwork but it was just mostly saddle them up, sack them out, and crawl on. Didn't have much handle on them the first time or two, and some of them could do a pretty fair job of bucking.

I watch those professional horse trainers now and I wonder, "why didn't I do it that way?" But then I believe each generation of horses are getting a little more buck bred out of them, which I figure also makes it easier.

I borrowed this story from J. Frank Dobie's Cow People and just made it rhyme.

Camp Meetin'

In the old days on the range,
when settlement was a sparse one,
a fellow drove his buggy up to a ranch,
told the folks there he was a parson.

Said he'd come to save some souls,
from their eternal damnation.
"He would do some right fine preachin',
if he could get him a congregation."

"Folks don't get much churchy edification,
'cause sermonizin' here is mighty slim.
Here's a preacher," the rancher thought,
"better get some preachin' out of him."

The rancher said "I can get you a crowd,
by sendin' some riders around.
And we'll put up a brush arbor,
for preachin', down on the river ground.

But I've got me just one question,
for you to answer, if you can.
Would you be a sheep man's preacher,
or do you sermonize to the cowman?"

The preacher, being a bright young man,
and not smelling, or seeing no sheep in sight.
Figured he'd better say cowman's preacher,
if he was going to answer it right.

Sunday, the preacher and the rancher's family
rode to the preachin' ground in a hack.
The rancher, partial to his own company,
followed them up a'straddle his old kack.*

Looking at cattle along the road
slowed him reaching the preachin' ground.
What he heard when he got there
made him turn right on around.

He got back on his horse and loped home,
just a'fuming all the way.
Feeling put upon and put out
by what he heard that preacher say.

"The Lord is my SHEPHERD" is what he heard.
Made him want to give that preacher a beatin'.
Here was a lying, sheepherder preacher,
preaching at a cow country camp meetin'.

* Kack - Saddle

You read about old-time traveling preachers. It wasn't easy being a preacher in those days, but they played a big roll in settling the west.

One story is told of a preacher coming into a town and the cowboys jeering him and making him dance by shooting close to his feet. He then said, "I danced for you fellows, now you are going to hear me preach. They gathered in the saloon where he proceeded to give them a lengthy sermon. They attentively listened to this man of God , with respect and admiration for his courage, taking up a collection when he was done.

Like Roy

When I was a Child my heroes
    were the toughest hombres I'd seen.
Those rootin' tootin' shootin' cowboys,
    ridin' hard across the screen.

Heck, Roy didn't mess with no stirrup
    when it come to gettin' on.
He vaulted over Trigger's rump,
    hit the saddle, and they were gone,

chasin' after bad men,
    and they never got away.
I was tough like Roy,
    in my imaginatin' play.

Rustlers came to know it didn't pay
    to be on the wrong side the law,
when I slapped leather
    in my lightnin' quick draw.

Ike Daltin came a'shootin' out the bank,
    sweet little Lil under his arm.
I had to stop that dastardly villain,
    before he did her harm.

Old Alpo, he was dozing,
    dreamin' horsey dreams no doubt.
He was startled some, to say the least,
    when I made my flyin' mount.

Guess I miscalculated my landin' zone,
    or launched with too much speed.
'cause I missed my intended spot,
    on the back of the steed.

When I went sailing over the saddle,
    I was thinkin' I had made a mistake.
Specially when the horn grabbed me,
    like a horseshoe snatchin' stake.

It bruised my... pride,
    and made an impression that'd last.
How could Roy, after his flyin' mount,
    ...always ride so fast.

I know an old cowboy who tells remarkable stories from the past. I never tire of listening to him.

This is one he told, said it was actually a true story. But then he also stated that, if he didn't exactly tell the truth, there wouldn't be anyone from that time who knew the difference, "cause they were all dead."

Stampede

There was a socialite from the east,
all lady and quite refined.
Who visited a western ranch,
and there she was to find

She liked the cowboy way of life,
and with the foreman was quite smitten.
She didn't know just how it happened,
but the love-bug had deeply bitten.

Now Tex was good at cowboy things,
but he had never tried no romance.
If she had her say, he wouldn't shy away,
she wasn't going to give him the chance.

She followed Tex around the ranch,
asking questions all the time.
She was interested in cowboy ways,
and her interest in Tex was on the climb.

She wanted to know all about ranch life,
and the things that cowboys do.
But mostly the reason she wanted to know,
was because he did those things too.

"I've heard about stampedes Tex,
and it must be a terrible fright.
When cattle run with wild abandon
and scatter into the night.

I know you have to get to work,
and are getting anxious to go.
But tell me Mr. Foreman Tex,
there's something I need to know.

I need to ask this question,
and will surely rely on your word.
But will just one critter stampede,
take off running like a whole herd?

Do they get as scared and run as fast,
get as crazy as a bunch and such?"
Tex slowly answered the eastern lady,
"yeah! ma'am, but they don't scatter as much."

I believe we, those of us who have an interest in writing, have an obligation to get the life stories of old-timers. Those folks have so much to tell of a much different time and different way of doing things. If these stories aren't recorded, they will be forever, irretrievably lost.

More than once, I figured on interviewing an old person but didn't get around to doing it, and then I heard that person had died. Another missed opportunity for a good story of the past that should have been written down for posterity.

My dad used to tell me stories, which he told as being true. I was a pretty gullible kid and I usually always believed him.

This is one of dad's stories and I don't know if it actually happened, but it surely could have, and probably did.

Rake Wreck

In the old days,
it was done a different way.
You hitched up horses,
when you needed to put up hay.

This here little episode, that
I'm about to relate to you,
was told to me by dad,
so I guess it must be true.

It seems Herman had some hay down,
and the hired man had left for good.
His wife, being a good wife,
said she'd do whatever she could.

So he put her on a dump rake,
to rake up some hay.
And this is the sad story,
of what happened that terrible day.

Now horses with broncy inclinations
were usually used on the rake.
Where an attitude adjustment,
didn't take long to make.

Herman was fiddlin' with the harness,
he was standing up ahead.
When the wind plucked the bonnet,
plumb off Mary's head.

37

It sailed through the air,
lit on one broad back.
That old pony thought for sure,
he was under a fearsome attack.

He took off running,
joined by his teammate.
Knocking Herman down,
under the rake.

They headed out across the meadow,
they were both running well.
Like they were being pursued,
by demons from hell.

He was rolling with the sandburs and hay,
she gripping the iron seat,
'cause she was scared to jump.
Old Herman was hollerin' for all he was worth,
"DUMP Mary, DUMP."

The hay rake was hard on horse's necks. The twelve-foot width of a rake caused the tongue to swing back and forth, thus jerking on the collars, making the horses necks sore. To prevent this, teams were usually hitched to a narrow wheeled cart and the rake was hooked to the cart.

We used to tie hard and fast (tie the end of the rope to the saddle horn) when heeling calves at a branding, which made for an occasional spectacular wreck.

Nowadays ropers dally the rope around the horn after they make a catch. This allows them to let go of the rope when they get in trouble.

Here are a couple scenarios that could happen from tying on.

Tyin' On

Jim had been a pretty good heel roper,
back in the days he was full of youthful sap.
But the sap had turned somewhat to syrup,
and he'd gotten too slow to take a wrap.

But age is overlooked by most cowboys,
as best they can, and its infirmities hid.
"Hell, experienced ropers tie on hard and fast,
dally'n' is for greenhorns and kids."

Now, tyin' to a critter does cause some wrecks,
as many a stifled cowboy tends to know.
But it's either tie on or just quit roping,
when a man he's getting way too slow.

He was dragging calves to the branding fire,
out roping all, doubling hocking, proud as punch.
His aches and pains plumb shucked away,
when he rode in on the big bunch.

The snorty baldy cow should have been sorted off,
but she was some proddy for sorting, anyway heck
she was staying outa the way so it surprised old Jim,
when his loop somehow settled... around her neck.

The cow was some surprised too, the tether
aggravating her already unsociable mood.

Suddenly Jim's tyin' on hard and fast,
as a thing to do, didn't seem so good.

She swung in a plunging symmetrical circle,
around the saddle-horn pivot point.
At the two o'clock spot of her raging arc,
the rope goosed Jim's horse, under the tail joint.

Old pony thought he was another Pegasus,
'cause he gave flying his best try.
Jim, he lost his hat, and then a stirrup.
Then he was on the ground wondering why

the gentle horse had thrown a fit,
why all the kids had learned to ride on him.
He was pondering the puzzling perplexity,
when the rampaging roped cow... run over Jim.

Or...

The cow got tired of her bellowing circle,
she changed her mind, and her course.
It wasn't a friendly bonding she had in mind,
when she headed for Jim's horse.

Jim was beginning to get the feeling,
felt by a fox chased goose.
He was wishing he had him some dallies,
he could sure-enough turn loose.

She hit the horse and slid on under,
Jim, like the skipper of a storm tossed ship,
could only figure on going down with his craft,
tied tightly to it, by the rope across his hip.

The cow was beginning to chock down some,
and she had lost a lot of her fight.
Jim, he was feeling mighty thankful,
that his horse had stayed upright.

A puncher cut the umbilical cord,
binding Jim to the cow.
Freedom had a new meaning for Jim,
and he was pondering now,

the wisdom of tying hard and fast,
when a man's got some roping to do.
And wondering if he maybe wasn't too old,
if he practiced taking his dallies too.

Chaps

My son Ken, and Jim Harms, have a heifer breeding busi-
ness that runs for several days each spring. They put
several folks heifers together, hire a crew and artificially
inseminate the cattle. It takes several riders and quite a
few saddle horses to sort the heifers as they come in heat.
I was helping them.

This one time they had steel cattle panels set up beside
the breeding chute, with an open end (don't ask me why),
where I was standing putting on my chaps.

Now, since I've gotten my way-past- middle-age spread,
my chaps have gotten pretty snug at the thighs, so it is
easier to start the zippers in a little more comfortable po-
sition and where I can see what I am doing. Then, I slide
them around, pull them up, and buckle and finish zipper-
ing them. I was in the process of doing this, standing at
the open end of the panels, when the chute crew turned
a heifer loose.

This particular black-baldy heifer was somewhat put out
by all the rear end prodding of her private parts. She
wasn't enjoying her impregnation at all and was, to put it
mildly, a mite peeved. I happened to be in just the right
position to be the first projected target for her anger.
I saw her coming and went to the opposite side of the
panel fence... where she followed me.

I climbed a panel, losing the hold on my chaps in the pro-
cess. Climbing a panel isn't easy with your chaps down
around your feet and an irate critter banging on your
butt.

I rolled over the top of the panel, scraping hide off one shin as I did so, and she came around the end to meet me. So over I went again, again with considerable incentive provided by her.

The heifer finally lost interest in this little one-sided punching bag game and went looking for another victim.

When I could concentrate on my surroundings, I noticed Ken, still standing on the panel fence, laughing so hard it was a wonder he didn't fall off. And Jim Harms, over by the chute, was doubled up on the ground, in imminent danger of busting a gut with his own laughter.

I didn't think it was anywhere near that funny.

Blue and I on the Aling crew.

My dad has been gone for forty years and had given up the use of all tobacco long before his passing.

One time when dad was horseback, he started to take a chew and got to thinking it was really a bad habit, so he put the lid back on the can and tossed it.

Several hours later I saw him riding, in widening circles, in the weeds, looking for that can of chew.

Later on, I started and then quit the bad habit so I know the feeling.

HOOKED

I toss and turn. I can't sleep,
I get up and walk the floor.
I'm yearning, burning and craving,
I've never wanted anything more.

Serum of need courses through my veins,
tortured thoughts, in my head.
Devilish, aching, raging lust,
relentlessly drives me from my bed.

I try to clear my head by thinking
of things like fun, drink and food.
Even thought of taking a cold shower,
but I knew it wouldn't do no good.

I want to do right, but guess I can't,
...kind of like that Jekyll and Hyde.
Ol' monkey's scratching and clawing,
and my guts are churning inside.

This senseless desire is driving me crazy.
I know now what I have to do.
I've got to go try to find the spot...
where I chucked that can of chew.

I figure being God gave us the horse to use, and being using the horse is the best possible way to handle cattle, then why not use a horse.

Four Wheeler Cowboys

In ranching, there's a goin'on I can't condone,
ranching is changing too fast, too much.
Some say "you've got to go with the flow,
that you've just got to keep in touch."

For sixty years I have straddled a saddle,
working cattle from the back of a horse.
Now modern ranchers say, "that's not the way,
there's a newer, better and faster way, of course."

When working cattle I know you have to go slow,
to avoid having one hell of a mess.
To keep cattle mild you don't do it wild,
those four wheeler gunsels couldn't care less.

If their gonna get it done, they'll do it on the run,
with those fast little noisy ATVs.
It's easy for them to say, "That is the way,"
in my mind, while runnin' pounds off their beeves.

I know, of course, they can't replace a horse,
to do the job right working cattle.
knowledge I share. ATV cowboys don't care.
I will keep doin' mine from the saddle.

If they would contemplate how, when cutting a cow,
the horse surely has it beat hands down.
They'd have to admit, some places ATVs ain't worth spit,
when it comes to getting around.

We had cows to sort, who thought it great sport
to go through a fence that needed repair.
So I, of course, rode over there on my horse,
my neighbor rode his four-wheeler there.

The sorting went good, better than I thought it would,
like working 'em in the home corral alley.
We'd covered some ground, so we looked around,
in order to get us a good final tally.

She was up to her belly, in water quite smelly.
Ah! This was my gloatin' time now.
I said, just as smug as a bug in a rug,
"Why don't you ride out and get that cow?"

*The ending of this story is completely factual. I, of course, drove
the cow out of the water.*

46

The Rancher

He sits upon his leather throne,
horn rubber wrapped, stamped Circle Y,
watching the cattle string past,
blacks, baldies, and some red.
The monarch of his piece of the land,
counting them as they go by.
A lifetime of work is in that herd,
four hundred and fifty head.

Dusty old hat pulled low,
shielding eyes from the setting sun.
As he counts he's watching
for something not quite right,
pink eye, lump jaw, a gimpy,
he could spot them on the run.
His livelihood depends on knowing,
and not much misses his sight.

He's watching to see how they're doing,
and if they've put on some gain.
Like with the cattle, his practiced eye,
surveys his Sandhills kingdom.
The chunk of land in his care,
his for awhile, in his reign.
Noticing where grass is ready for grazing,
and where it needs to grow some.

He don't need someone telling him,
he's got to take care of the land.
Those who say he's ruining the earth are wrong,
and his view of them is dim.
The land is where he makes his living,
and the land's where he wants to live.
He knows if he don't take care of it,
it ain't going to take care of him.

Trailin' to Grass

The early mornin's sharpened my old pony's senses keen.
And he's doin' some snortin', at shadows not yet seen.

I speak softly to him, as I pull the latigo tight.
Waiting for the dawn, to chase away the night.

I hear good natured grumbling, from the cowboys sad-
dlin' up.
"Most folks do their work sometime after sunup."

A long hard winter's over, spring has come at last.
And it's time to trail the cows and calves to grass.

We're out the gate at daylight, headed on up through the
pass.
Those cows don't need no proddin', 'cause they're goin'
out to grass.

I slouch some in the saddle, Ol' Smoke, he knows the way.
And I'm thankin' the creator, for makin' such a perfect
day.

I've been trailin' cattle to grass, nigh onto seventy years.
Just a another part of ranching, a part that I hold dear.

I'm storin' and hangin' onto these memories that are
mine.
Oh! Lord, let me trail to grass, just one more time.

Spot

When I was a kid I wasn't wanting to be anything but a cowboy when I grew up. In the meantime I had to go to school, which I figured wasn't real necessary because cowboys didn't go to school, but my parents didn't seem to agree with that line of thinking.

The school I attended was a one-room country school, and the way my sister and I got there was by horseback, the horse spending the day in a little shed in the corner of the schoolyard. But being from a family not over blessed with possessions just one horse could be spared for our transportation, so we rode double my sister behind the saddle carrying the lard buckets containing our lunch.

Spot.

Old Spot was a docile plodding creature. Her, much practiced, motherly instinct seemed to kick in when we, and an assortment of cousins had learned to ride on her, and she took care of us. Always gentle and dependable, you could pile as many kids on her as would fit.

But Spot had a weakness, extra sensitive flanks and, despite her gentleness, a wayward heel coming in tickling contact with that portion of her anatomy would sometimes cause her to react by attempting to buck, the effort a comical ineffectual crow hop.

It was a warm spring day when school let out so all the kids were out in the yard when we mounted up.... What a chance to show off my long-suppressed cowboy skills. I kicked Old Spot's ribs, in preparation for a running exit, startling her from her usually vegetative state and causing her to jump, thereby causing my sister, gamely hanging on to the cantle and the lunch buckets, to bounce, causing each foot to thump a flank, causing Old Spot to summon up enough energy for her best imitation of a buck.

The upshot of the whole deal was I made a heck of a bronc ride and left the schoolyard at a fast run, at least as fast as Old Spot could run. My sister and the lunch buckets were still in the schoolyard, but I didn't know it. I was cowboying and I had the attention of the whole passel of kids. I had gone maybe a hundred yards when a couple gals, who lived close to the school and happened to be riding by, chased me down and sent me back after my sister.

She was a mite peeved.

Underwear Undoin'

In the old days on the range,
long ago, way back when.
The living was mighty tough,
and men were danged sure men.

The land it sorely tried them,
and it whipped a few.
It was hell on horses and women,
so they had to be formidable too.

Ike and Slim and Jake were
riding back from a cattle drive.
They was plumb tuckered out,
having hit the saddle before five.

They were riding Injun silent,
thinking about bedding for the night.
When they rode up over a hill,
and a ranch house hove in sight.

With seeing a possible haven,
Ike's spirits began to soar.
Comedian, prankster, of the trio,
he figured he'd pull one more.

"Jake's horse looks a might droopy,
s'pose there's some life left in him."
With a wicked grin he uncoiled his rope,
and tossed one end to Slim.

Jake was dozing in the saddle,
the old pony ambling down the trail.
When his partners raced on by,
Jerking the rope under the horse's tail.

Jake survived the dastardly attack.
and he was doing right fine.
He hadn't yet grabbed leather...
when they went under the clothesline.

The lady had just hung her wash
before the buckin' binge.
In her laundry was a bunch of
...not cowboy type under things.

Jake fit him a pretty good ride,
looked like he was going to get by.
But he was handicapped some, riding blind,
with the lingerie covering his eyes.

And when he lost a stirrup,
ol' Jake, he lost the race.
He settled blissfully to sleep,
with them undies clinging to his face.

Jake unfurled his banner
as he struggled to his knees.
In wondrous awe he stuttered,
"it'd t-t-take a lot a woman gonna fill these."

What Not to Rope

Lately my desire to be a good roper seems to have gotten to be directly correlated to the size of the critter needing roped. I mean, knowing I have to do something with whatever I rope kinda puts a damper on my roping ability.

It had been a pretty good calving season. I'd had very little death loss and hadn't, up to branding, doctored a sick calf. Then we got a wet spell and with it some scours and a little pneumonia.

I have always started calving in early February, so by pasture time, those calves weighed more than I do and had a blamed-site more energy. And I am increasingly getting acquainted with the fact that handling those big calves does often exact a toll. So, if I had to catch one, my heart just wasn't in it.

Anyway my grandson came out from town, and we doctored anything that even looked like it was thinking of getting the scours. At that time Tyler was a big, strapping teenager, and a high-school wrestler to boot; so I figured he might as well get some more practice on those calves.

When the cows and calves were bunched for caking, and I didn't figure there was enough calves needing attention to take a horse out, I would walk through them with my pockets full of necessary medical stuff, and carry a rope. I could usually heel a calf without scattering the herd. That works pretty well when the calves are small.

Awhile after we had gone through the bunch, I was checking them when I ran across what was probably the earliest calf in the herd. He had droopy ears and a dry nose and looked like a genuine pneumonia case.

Now, when I tie onto a husky calf, I prefer to be horseback but being I was afoot, I had it in mind that I would dally the rope on the trailer hitch ball, once I got him caught. I worked him in close to the pickup and snagged a hind foot. Right there is where my plan kinda fell apart.

The calf wasn't near as sickly as he looked, and I missed the pickup by several rope lengths as he headed down hill. But I had the calf, and he had my rope, and I wasn't wanting to lose either one. I went with him, traveling much faster and stepping a whole lot higher than I usually do. Our errant course took us past an REA pole at the bottom of the hill, and I managed to grab a quick dally and stop the runaway.

There was, of course, a depression around the pole, and it was, of course, filled with water. Therefore, my boots were full of water too. When I got to where I could partially breath again, I gave the calf a shot. I'm convinced I was in worse condition, after doctoring that calf, then he was to begin with.

One thing about it, when one of those big calves is needin' doctorin', thinkin' about it ain't gonna get the job done. I think it was Mark Twain who offered this bit of advice, *"If you've got a frog to swaller, don't look at it too long."*

The Blizzard

In the morning, it began, a soft, gentle snow.
Then from out of the east, a light breeze began to blow.

At twenty degrees, 'till about noon, then the temperature
plummeted down.
It started snowing harder, and the wind shifted around

into the north, and came up. The cattle and ranchers
knew,
from instinct and experience, a bad blizzard was in the
brew.

Around four that afternoon, out of the northwest, it came
in.
The swirling, drifting snow, pushed by a shrieking wind.

On the telephone line, a chilling frantic plea, from a
rancher's wife, her husband had left at three.

Rode out to hunt some cattle that had drifted with the
snow. To find him they knew was hopeless, but his neigh-
bors had to go.

Not cowardice turned them back, those ranchers had
plenty of sand.
But in that swirling white hell, you couldn't see the back
of your hand.

Two days, three nights it raged, like a pain crazed, mad
whelp.
They knew he had found shelter, or was beyond human
help.

The storm died at daybreak, the day bright with sunshine.
The neighbors began a search, dreading what they would
find.

They found the cattle first, where they figured at the start.
And the way that they found them, would chill any cattle-
man's heart.

Drifted in a fence corner, carcasses stacked like firewood .
And on the outer edge, a living skeleton stood.

A cow with frozen feet, she would never walk again.
Blinded by the clinging ice, beyond the feel of pain.

When they found him, the sight in their minds forever
would abide.
A still standing frozen horse, the dead man leaning
against its side.

The horse had tried to get them home, against a wire
fence it did stand.
Too far gone to get them through, the rider's cold numbed
mind and hands.

The blizzard brought moisture for the new spring grass to
grow.
The ever-warming sun, soon melted all the snow.

And not a trace remained, of that terrible killing snow.
But a pile of bleaching bones, and a grieving, heart sick
widow

It had been dry for quite awhile in the Sandhills. The summer of 2003 was particularly bad, dry and hot. We didn't get enough rain that spring to make a decent hay crop and the pastures went fast. Some said it was as bad as in the dirty thirties, others said it wasn't. I wasn't old enough then to know anything about that.

Drouth

Oh God! It's hot,
and so terrible dry.
I look at the parched land,
and I wonder why

it has to be this way.
Why there has to be this pain
in the eyes of folks of the land.
"Oh Lord, why don't it rain?"

It's dryer than it's been for long,
in fact since the thirties they tell.
I was too young to really remember,
but older folks recall that time well.

They talk about scanning the sky
for rain bearing clouds each day.
And of the hopeless despair
of watching those clouds drift away.

They speak of grasshoppers and dust,
in that time it was so dry,
of thirsty, thin listless cattle,
and watching their crops wither and die.

They tell about the hard struggle,
of just trying to hang on.
And they tell about packing it in,
picking up, and moving on.

They tell about hard times of the thirties,
and they say it could be happening again.
And they tell about rebirth of the land,
when it finally began to rain.

When I was a kid we didn't have a trailer to haul our horses around. I suppose other ranches had a trailer, but we didn't. I didn't even know anyone who had a trailer.

When we drove cattle somewhere, no matter how far or what time we got there, when we got done doing whatever we were doing with the cattle, we mounted up and rode home. There were times it was pitch black dark long before we got there.

Cowboy Poetry Gathering

From the Sandhills to the flinthills,
from desert to high country.
They come to communicate and orate,
if their yarns aren't true they could be.

They tell about dishonesty and loyalty,
and riding for the brand,
about trying and about dying,
and about making a pretty good hand.

About aching, and about breaking,
about good horses and bad rides.
About yearning and about learning,
and they talk about cowboy pride.

About hurtin' loves and soiled doves,
and good cowboys gone wrong.
They reminisce in poetic bliss,
in metered rhyming verse and song.

You'll find cowboys and plowboys
at a gatherin', maybe a sheepherder or two.
Even urban wives, fellows who wear ties,
Yeah! They're wanting to be country to.

Poetry's the thing that tends to bring
these folks together from time to time.
They've a story to tell, and they do it well,
as long as they can do it in rhyme.

Snubbin' Post

Long ago the snubbin' post, it gave up the ghost,
like so many things from the past.
Old-timers will tell that it's just as well,
some old ways don't last.

Weathered and grooved, worn shiny smooth,
from countless coils of hemp.
Snubbin' post dues was many a bruise,
in a wild and woolly attempt
to subdue a cow, those old boys knew how,
needin' doctorin', or a sawed off horn.
From that hard strain, in some cowboy's brain,
...the idea of the squeeze chute was born.

*We have roped our calves at branding time ever since we moved
to the place south of Wood Lake, but most of the neighbors didn't. The
procedure was to put the calves in a small pen, a wrestler would drag
the calf out by a hind leg, his partner would get hold of the front end
and throw the calf. Or they would hold the calf down in the pen, which
sometimes got kind of crowded with the calves pressing in.*

*It took awhile for them to start roping their calves but, going to
brandings where that was done, they could see that it was easier on
the wrestlers and a lot faster. Very few ranches in this part of the coun-
try don't rope now*

*On bigger ranches they have two openings in a large portable
corral, with two complete crews. There are four or more roping, each
dragging a calf out the closest opening to up to a half dozen sets of
wrestlers. A lot of calves can be branded in not a lot of time.*

Cowboy Streakers

Now Slim and Ed were tight, drinkin' most all night,
and they got to talking about all the injustice being done.
They'd allow as how that needed to be settled... now.
They had to do something, but could think of only one

thing to do to make a point. So before they left the beer
    joint,
they formulated their ingenious plan of protestation.
They would sneak in, take their clothes off and do some
    streakin',
and get on the prime-time news all around the nation.

A July Fourth rodeo was held each year, and the time was
    here.
Slim and Ed rehashed their protesting plans.
After the grand entrance would come their time to dance,
in front of all those people in the stands.

They shucked their duds in back of the little entry shack,
but then they got to serious thinkin' that
since they'd never gone barefooted they'd best remain
    booted,
and they wouldn't think of running without a hat.

These two old Waddies, when unclothed, their bodies
would have been a portrait painters nightmare.
But it helped their cause, the old boys thought, because
their pasty-white bodies would easy be seen there.

Their run was a speedy burst, at least it was the first
fifty feet, runnin' in their birthday suit.
Though he was game, Ed was getting winded and lame
by the time they got to the ropin' chute.

Their streakin' had effect, not the way that they'd expect,
they made the local news, the crowd noticed them for
    sure
They spent a night in jail, 'till their wives put up the bail.
Sadly, their daring protesting run didn't cure

any worldly ill, the old boys thought but still,
they'd be proud to have it on their epitaph,
that they set out to do what they figured they had to,
and they gave the rodeo crowd a good laugh.

I wrote this at the time of the controversy over the government's proposed mandatory animal identification, which very few ranchers thought was necessary.

Animal ID

For maybe thousands of years
folks have used a system well tried,
to claim ownership of a critter,
by burning a brand on its hide.

And that worked pretty good,
with a minimum of strife.
The brand proved ownership
throughout the critters life.

Then Uncle Sam got involved,
and he don't know diddily squat.
He wants to do it some different,
that, it looks like, will cost a lot.

He says, as proper identification,
the brand won't work no more.
So in order to keep tract of cattle,
he's got some changes in store.

Like computerized ear tags,
or putting a chip under the hide.
A brand still seems a better way to me,
because you can see it, on the outside.

I understand you read the data
by waving a little fairy wand.
I know a lot about old ranchers,
and they ain't gonna want to respond

to this frivolous use of technology,
that's bound to be strife with many flaw.
I'll bet they're just not quite meekly
going to go with the government law.

To those cowmen, government employs
just wouldn't start to make the cut.
And I'd sure be willing to bet,
they'd like to brand some government butt!

When the government decides it wants to do something, it doesn't really matter if it has to walk on some one to get it done. There was a big push for premise identification, which went hand in hand with animal ID.

It even came down to taking away the rights of children involved in 4-H, if their parents didn't register their premise. I received two or three letters and filed them in the trashcan, figuring the government is already trying to keep too close of tabs on its citizens. After pressure from a cattle group, they made premise identification voluntary.

I realize part of the reason for premise identification is to track disease, but they have been doing pretty good at finding where mad cow infected critters, from Canada, ended up in the U.S. One wag suggested the government ought to give a cow to each potential terrorist who slips into the country. "It would make them easier to find."

Brassiere Buyin'

He had been cowboyin'
since Shep was a pup.
Ridin' broncs or ropin' bulls,
he could surely cowboy up.

He could handle 'bout anything,
wasn't much could put him down.
But he finally met his match,
just on a trip to town.

He knew he was in trouble,
when his wife of twenty year.
Mentioned, as he was leaving,
that she needed a new brassiere.

Said, "since he was headed for town,
and she wouldn't be going for awhile,
that he might as well pick one up,
the Firmer Fitting Foundation Style."

He knew he had best do it,
if he wanted to keep on eatin'.
But rather than enter that store,
he'd just as soon take a beatin'.

A lady met him at the door,
all smiles and fancy dressed.
He looked down at his scuffed boots
and he was feelin' right depressed.

The shoppers in the store that day,
were eyein' him with glee.
Seemed they got some amusement
from his bra buyin' spree.

He wanted to get it over with,
and get back out of that store.
He knew one thing for sure,
he wasn't comin' back no more.

He said to the lady "My wife,
she's thinkin' she needs a new riggin'
She says she wants it to fit,
so it'll likely need to be a big'n."

"I'm sure I can help you sir
lingerie is what were all about.
Now... **what bust**?" "Uh, didn't bust
at all ma'am. It just plumb wore out."

Jack

I would be remiss if I didn't mention, in this book about cowboys, my brother Jack. He was darn sure a cowboy. There wasn't any part of cowboying Jack wasn't good at, on the ranch or in the arena.

Jack's specialty was riding bulls. He won quite a few buckles and was runner up to the mid-states champion two years. He went into the finals both times with a comfortable lead, but injuries kept the championship just out of his grasp.

The injury was pretty serious the last time. He drew a bull that had few qualified rides on him. Jack was dragged off by the chute gate and hung up in his rope. The bull had broken a horn off the night before and swung his head, hitting Jack's cheekbone with the jagged stub. Jack was in the hospital a long time and, though he died quite a few years later, of an aneurysm at age forty-six, I have always contributed his death to that wreck.

Jack won the bull riding on the last bull he got on, at the Old Timers Rodeo, at Hyannis, Nebraska. His wife facetiously said he couldn't get out of bed for two days afterward.

When Jack quit riding bulls he took up steer wrestling and did pretty good at that. Then he started team roping, roping the heels. Again, that was something he was good at.

I saw Jack try to ride a saddle bronc once. I think that was the only time he entered that competition. He got planted hard, just outside the chute, and, I suppose, that might have been enough to convince him that he might not have been a saddle bronc rider, though he did get on some barebacks.

Jack traveled the state for several years rodeoing and I remember sometimes feeling a bit resentful because he was off rodeoing while I was home doing the work. But I am glad he did that, especially since he enjoyed it and especially because he died at such a young age.

A common ordinary life just wouldn't have fit Jack at all.

More than a Chip Off the Block

There wasn't much keeping him on,
'cept hanging tough and a will to stay.
It wasn't very much pretty to watch,
but the kid was riding that little bay.

It's a fact, he was riding all over the saddle,
and would of bucked off a time or two,
if that pony hadn't come back under him.
Grit and determination was showing through.

He grabbed for leather more than once
then changed his mind before the fact.
I tell you that kid on that bay pony,
though not fancy, was still a class act.

As I stood watching that young bronc rider,
my heart was near busting with pride.
Pride in him wanting to be like his dad,
but mostly because my son could ride.

In very few occupations, other than ranching, a father and son get to work together. I sincerely believe that gives country kids a head start over those born and raised in the city.

Even when the father and son, or daughter, don't get along all that good the kids are learning to do something worthwhile, and they are learning responsibility, which generally is a benefit to them as adults.

Hat

He wore that hat when it was new,
neat and fresh as his young life.
He wore it when courting the girl,
that was to become his wife.

He'd tossed the hat on the curly head,
of a bright eyed cowpuncher lad,
who couldn't think of anything,
but growing up to be like his dad.

He had held that hat to his breast,
and tightly gripped the brim.
At the burial of a young cowboy,
who had been like a brother to him.

He's worn that hat to church,
sharp, shaped just right, and perk.
It's just an old work hat now,
covered with blood, stains and dirt.

The old hat's seen better days,
and it looks like it is near its end.
But it's been with him so long,
it is kind of like a good friend.

He has worn that hat proud,
proud of what he's been.
And going back along his life,
he would do it all over again.

Looks Like Rain

"Looks like rain" he said, hitching his pants,
as he scanned the morning sky.
"Think we're gonna get a little shower,
if them clouds don't drift on by."

"It's been some dry
for quite a spell.
Gonna hafta rain
to get grass, but hell,

it's always rained before,
and likely will again.
Ain't gettin' no guarantee
just exactly when."

He thinks of another dry time,
when calves slipped to 34 cents.
When he sold them that fall,
he'd come up short on his rent.

And his thoughts take him back,
to the dry spring of eighty-four.
He lost his partner that summer,
so he don't like thinking of it no more.

The going had been tough
when she hit her bad spell.
Those ends weren't coming nowhere close,
so he knew he'd have to sell.

The folks down at the bank
had finally called in his loan.
He wishes he could have held onto the cows,
until after she was gone.

They hadn't had no kids,
he don't rightly know why.
And lonely comes a spurrin',
as he squints at the sky.

Another time, another man's place
is where he calls home.
But he takes care of the cattle,
like they were his own.

And he tries not remembering bad times,
helps him shy away from the pain.
He does most his thinking on good things.
"Yeah! Looks like it's gonna rain."

Cancer took my wife in 1986 and the ranch was a terrible big and lonely place afterwards. This poem is from that time and though the situation was some different, the emotions brought in the poem by losing a mate are so much real. As are the painful emotions of thinking of all the things you should have done when she was here.

Only one who has been there can know of the intense emotions that follow the loss of a spouse, not only sorrow, but anger... sometimes at her, for leaving.

Last Ride

The preacher is sayin' he's better off,
'cause he's gone to a better place, you see.
Martha's cryin' and carryin' on,
and I'm thinkin' she don't agree.

The boys are fidgetin' there in the pew,
some spooked by that preacher man.
And knowin' wherever it is he's goin',
they're getting them a real good hand.

They got him all gussied up,
layin' there on that satin pall.
I reckon they done their best,
but it don't look like him at all.

Shoot, he's even wearin' a suit.
Ain't seen him duded up none that I know.
'cept when him and Martha got hitched
must been 'round thirty years ago.

We rode together now and then,
on spreads both sides the divide.
He was a man you'd want at your back,
and a friend to have by your side.

He was a cowman and a cowboy,
hell of a bronc rider, doncha know.
Don't know how far he coulda gone
if he'd chosen to rodeo.

We hit a few, him and me,
back in our younger days.
I was just along for the ride,
he was makin' it pay.

He mostly rode a company's string,
ridin' for wages, a hired hand.
Wherever it was that he worked,
he damn sure rode for the brand.

Him and Martha had scraped together
a chunk of land of their own.
Wasn't much, just a little place,
they could settle on and call home.

He'd had some wrecks from time to time,
some laid him up for awhile.
He'd grin and say "can't keep me down,
I'm good for quite a few mile."

Wasn't a wreck that put him down
a wreck he could understand.
Not this thing that grows and eats,
at the insides of a man.

He'd took some bad rides,
hung on when the chips were down.
He knew from the start he wasn't going
to get to win this go 'round.

He didn't die with his boots on,
I know if he'd had his say.
When he took that final ride,
he would of done it the cowboy way.

Tony and Topsy

There were a whole lot of things my sister and I didn't have when we were kids, but we didn't know we didn't have them. There was something we had though that made up for a lot of not having the other stuff.

My sister was (and is) a little over a year younger than I and when I was probably eight or nine dad bought a pony for each of us.

Those ponies, Tony and Topsy, weren't little bitty ornery ponies but half Shetland, the size of a small saddle horse and pretty good little cow horses. We rode them every day when the weather was decent, usually bareback, and on the run a good share of the time.

We would play Cowboy and Indian, shooting each other off the back of a running pony. We threw our arms up and rolled off the pony just like in the movies. The ponies always waited for us so we could get back on.

We practiced standing on the pony's backs, barefooted, traveling them side-by-side down a trail road. We fell off a lot but we got so we could run those ponies, standing on their backs and the ponies got so they would travel together at an even stride..

About every fall we rode Tony and Topsy to the Brown County Fair and entered them in the races, riding bareback. The ponies were fast, usually winning when competing against horses their size and could outrun a lot of saddle horses.

My mother taught country schools and before my younger brother, Jack, started school, dad kept him home while mom was teaching. Dad hunted coyotes, following the hounds on horseback. He would mount Jack on old Tony and they followed dad on a hard run when they jumped a coyote, maybe one or two hills behind but coming strong.

I have ridden a lot of good horses through the years, some I remember better than others. But I well remember Tony and Topsy. We had a lot of fun with them and, riding bareback, I got to be a pretty good rider.

Topsy and I.

Ranching isn't just an occupation, it is a way of life. One has to want to be doing that or he wouldn't. The work is harder than in most, the financial reward is too often lacking, and....

S'pose I Coulda Lived in the City

Sometimes I get to thinking,
life, it ain't been all that good.
It should have been some easier,
and then I recollect it could

be my fate to have lived in L.A.,
Denver, DesMoines or Chicago.
Crowded in a concrete jungle,
and then I would never know

the easy gaited good feel of a horse,
breaking into a long strided lope.
I wouldn't be knowing horse sense savvy,
and I'd not learned to handle a rope.

I wouldn't know the satisfaction
of seeing a calf take its first meal.
I'd never known the heartache and pain,
that comes from having to deal

with sickness and death invading the herd,
to which all my hopes and plans are tied.
When all I could do just wasn't enough,
didn't seem to matter how hard I tried.

I couldn't see the sun break over the ridge,
or smell clean earth after a summer rain.
I wouldn't have known long lonely quite,
and I couldn't have had a chance to train

my young ones in the way of the range,
and watch each, their skills perfect.
And see them come to care for the land,
as I, with love and nurturing respect.

I couldn't lean over the corral fence,
just gazing out across the land.
Feeling free and mighty thankful,
and thinking, and trying to understand

how folks could live all crowded up,
like a bunch of cattle in a pen.
Seems like they'd get plumb proddy
and want to break out. But then

I get to thinking that's good,
anyway far as I can see.
Folks stay packed in their cities.
it leaves more room for me.

If I'd lived in the city, I wouldn't know the pride
in a hard day's work on my own place.
And fretting about all left undone,
when I couldn't keep up the pace.

I couldn't have heard a coyote howl,
or heard a meadowlark sing.
I wouldn't have had concern for cattle,
that raging snowstorms bring.

I wouldn't have known the serenity
of watching long evening shadows change.
And challenge the heat of a summer day,
as twilight lays claim to the range.

Bronc Riders

Now, cowboys are noted for braggin' ability,
in tellin' about the rough horses they've rode.
And the rides get better each and every tellin',
that just seems to be the cowboy code.

He don't have to be a rodeo hand,
just a ranch waddy; doin' his job.
He tells of sitting with ease and spurrin',
the bronc was always rougher'n a cob.

Don't matter what shape the cowboy was in,
young or old, fat or thin, short or tall.
When it come to stompin' a bronc,
that didn't really enter into it at all.

He could always stay on top,
of a kicken', sunfishin' sun of a gun.
According to him, the harder the buck,
the more he was startin' to have fun.

Of fellows that didn't make the ride,
he laughs and jeers and scoffs.
But he don't talk at all about
the times that he bucked off.

If you see your stirrups slap together above your saddle horn, you're probably bucked off.

New Beginning

The brown winter grass
sparkles with early morning frost.
The trees stand stark and bare,
victims to winter's long cold cost.

The land lies still and dormant,
under harsh winter's icy chill.
Then a bit of green can be seen,
peeking from the side of a hill.

It bursts in panoramic grandeur.
A wondrous carpet of new grass.
A resurrection of new beginning,
as the trying times of winter pass.

The trees regain their stately beauty,
and melodious bird songs fill the air.
On one of the ponds in the meadow
two geese are floating, a mating pair.

The clear sky goes on forever,
life is geared to rhythm of the land.
Sunshine is gaining strength,
warming the many hills of sand.

Nature is awakening renewed,
bestowing her flowers and frills.
A carpet of serenity and beauty,
across Nebraska's vast Sandhills.

Ridin' Drag

On the north end of a southbound herd,
chousin' up critters that lag.
You'll find the greenhorns and kids,
back in the rear, ridin' drag.

When the trail drive lines out,
all know where they're supposed to ride.
The boss and the old hands take point,
and they ride along each side.

You get to feelin' put out,
and put upon somehow.
And plumb sick of lookin'
at the tail end of a cow.

You'd like to cowboy up,
'cause you've been inclined to brag.
But you can't show your stuff,
back there ridin' drag.

You know you'd do all right
if you was ridin' up ahead.
You mentioned this to the boss,
but he just shook his head.

"That could maybe be," he said,
"but I need you right here,
trailin' along behind the herd,
bringin' up the rear."

Sometimes it seems life,
it ain't quite just.
Way back there behind the herd,
eatin' all that dust.

But life is like a trail drive,
remember that when spirits sag.
Someday you'll be ridin' point,
and the greenhorns and kids ridin' drag.

When you are riding point you need to look back from time to time to make sure the herd is still there.

Always drink upstream from the herd.

I never did get on a bull. I would occasionally get a fleeting notion that I should enter the bull riding, but just couldn't talk myself into it. I don't know if it was because I was long on sense or short on guts.

No Pain, No Gain

I was watchin' bull ridin' wrecks
one night. I think it was on CMT.
And, bein' under a big angry bull,
didn't look like where I'd wanta be.

The bull riders talked of all can happen,
when tied on a bull when he bucks.
And if you didn't get injured at all,
you'd be packin' some kind of luck.

They know they'll be carried out on a board.
They figure it's just a matter of time.
But they're gonna give it all they've got,
while they're still in their bull ridin' prime.

They told about the hurts they'd had,
in some of their bull ridin' wrecks.
About broken arms, and noses and teeth,
and ankles, ribs, and busted necks.

About shoulders jammed and dislocated,
and bruises, sprains and concussions too.
And in gettin' healed up so they can ride
again, they'll do what they have to do.

They're sure not wantin' to get hurt,
But the thought don't slow them down.
They'll deal with it the best they can,
when that time rolls around.

They allowed as how the best bull riders,
have a better chance of stayin' intact.
But agreed that skill's no guarantee,
while tryin' to stay on a mad bull's back

They reminisced about good friends
who would never ride again.
They spoke of bull ridin' philosophy,
"Ain't no pain – no gain."

Rodeoing has changed drastically. Not only has the, bred to buck, stock gotten rougher but rodeo winnings are a whole lot better.

I try to watch, via television, at least part of the National Finals Rodeo and it amazes me how hard those horses and bulls buck, and how good the riders are who are mounted on them. I am also impressed with what a rodeo cowboy can win nowadays. I watched Justin McBride win two hundred thousand dollars on a matched bull ride, matched between him and the bull.

The mid-states rodeos are paying a significant deal more now. I do realize that everyone is getting paid more for what they do now, but just to show a comparison... After winning third place on a bareback horse, a long long time ago, I received a check for twenty-eight dollars. I don't remember what my entry fee was.

Change

Where the branding corral was
is just tangled rusting wire.
Most of the posts are gone,
consumed by rot and prairie fire.

Paint is peeling from the house
the windows broken, shingles are loose.
A sad testimony of abandoned neglect,
when a home is no longer in use.

The barn, like a tired old man,
leans more with each high wind.
The board siding is warped and gray,
part of the steep roof has fallen in.

Down the winding road a ways
there is a mansion on a hill.
Put there for a part time home,
a big house but no ranching skill.

That place had known four generations
then it fell upon a hard time.
It has another owner now,
who came from a different clime.

A clime of big corporate dealings,
maybe some not above the board.
Dealings worth a lot of money,
that allowed him to hoard

to afford to buy the land of his choice,
and build a fancy dwelling there.
About the way of life of the neighbors,
he just doesn't know or care.

But he has his big ranch,
and is a rancher in his mind.
I'm sitting here and thinking,
"we really don't need that kind."

Starting at the Top

I've been a cowboy all my life,
everything I do involves a cow.
I'd like to climb the economic ladder,
but I don't rightly know how.

I ride a lot, and I work hard,
I put in long hours too.
I don't really mind that, but
I'd like more pay for what I do.

I see the bankers and CEOs,
see them live a life of ease.
I don't know how to go about it,
but if I could just, please,

have a little bit of all that
money that they've got.
Just some of it would do,
I wouldn't have to have a lot.

I know it would be a hard climb,
to get to where they are.
I sit here sad and thinkin',
there's no way I could get that far.

I'd be willing to start at the bottom,
and slowly work my way on up.
But I'm thinkin' my chances wouldn't be
any better than that of a stray pup.

I don't doubt, at bankin' or CEOn',
I would surely be a flop.
Guess I'll take a job diggin' postholes.
That way I can start at the top.

The Ranching Blues

I wanted to come to your gathering,
it sounds like a real good time.
Even went in on my computer,
and looked it up online.

I know you offered to pay me some,
and put me up in a motel.
I was really looking forward to coming,
but, right now, I'm not doing so well.

Things here aren't working out
like I had hoped they would.
And the chances of making it next fall,
they just aren't looking so good

Tractor quit when I was putting up hay,
they said they'd need to keep it a spell.
Meanwhile my mowed alfalfa
was getting 'bout dryer than... hell.

Hay wasn't too good to start with,
and I grow a hay crop for cash.
Saying I was gonna come out in the hole,
I guess, wouldn't be too awful rash.

My wife's car needs repair. Fuel
price keeps going up. That's not all.
My son just headed for the city,
he's starting college this fall.

Looks like I can't afford to come,
the way things are around here.
Appreciate if you would keep me in mind,
and call me again next year.

Where Do Cowboy Go When They Die

Montana rancher, Wally McCrae, wrote a poem sometime ago about cowboys and reincarnation. In the poem a cowboy asks about reincarnation so his friend creates a scenario on how he thought the cowboy would return in his reincarnated form.

The cowboy dies and is buried and enriches the soil, a flower grows and a horse comes along and eats the flower. A little bit nourishes the horse and the rest passes on through. So he says "I come upon the site and sees what the horse left." He allowed as how he'd figure the old boy hadn't changed all that much.

In a song the question is asked, "Where do cowboys go when they die?"

I was taking a bunch of heifers out to pasture and had to do some hard riding to get them out the gate off the flat, headed the right way through the hills and to get ahead of them to open the gate into the pasture and drive them through it.

When I got them strung out, headed down a valley to the well, my dog was trotting along behind them and Old Blue was settled down, walking sensible. It was a clear spring day which would have been hot except for a cool breeze, not the infernal, nerve wracking wind we frequently get, but just enough to turn the windmills, the rare kind of a spring day when you are dressed just right to be completely comfortable, the kind of day that makes up for a bunch of bad ones. As I relaxed in the saddle I thought, "It just doesn't get much better than this."

There is something about springtime in the Sandhills that renews a fellow's lease on life, bolsters sagging spirits, makes him seem more sound in body and mind and even seems to roll back the years. I Couldn't help thinking of how thankful I should be to have lived in the Sandhills in the springtime.

I think that has something to do with pride. Life in the Sandhills allows us the freedom of individuality, not to be just another number and face in the crowd. And we can be proud of our roll in perpetuating a culture which, though it has changed immensely, has in some ways remained basically the same for generations.

But I suppose we Sandhillers don't have an edge on pride. I imagine there are a lot of ranchers, in many places, sitting on a horse, looking out across their land and thinking, "It just don't get no better." I have a poem I wrote that starts out:

I would like heaven to be a little bit of each pretty place I have seen.

I don't want to walk on streets of gold, but on grass that is always green.

Spike Van Cleve spoke of that pride when he wrote in Forty Years Gatherins'. "Somehow the hereafter is the least of my worries. It's a cinch I'll foregather with more than a few of my friends in hell, if I end up there. If not, what could be finer than a bright spring day in lovely country, at a long lope on a good horse, with the wind in my face. Hell, I've already had heaven."

When you can look back over your life and know in your heart that it was a ride you'd take all over again, I think you've lived a full, satisfying life. You are truly blessed.

Jonathan D. Finck

Taking Five

They've finished branding the first bunch.
The roundup crew is bringing in some more.
The cowboys are gathered 'round the pump,
taking five, drinking, talking and resting before

they tackle the next gather of calves.
They're laughing, joshing and poking fun.
"Tom, was you heelin' calves or fishin'.
I thought you was a roper, old son."

The horses are getting a breather too,
reins loose wrapped, standing at ease.
Tight latigos loosened a couple holes,
they're cooling in the morning breeze.

The white stocking sorrel, standing hip shod,
he's sure enough earned his rest.
Of the good horses in cattle country,
the cowboys all know he's the best

Just a little bit shy of sixteen hands,
with twelve years under the saddle.
The old pony knows all he needs to know,
when it has something to do with cattle.

He's been dragging calves all morning,
he's glad to stand, taking five.
Resting, and dozing, and waiting,
waiting for the next bunch to arrive.

"Look back at our struggle for freedom, trace our present day's strength to the source; and you will find that man's pathway to glory is strewn with the bones of a horse."

I wrote this and the previous poem for a poster poem contest for the Durango Gathering. They sent the poster two different years and I had to write a poem to march the theme portrayed by the artist

Doing Winter Work

It comes in from the north, the wind driven snow.
The temperature, it drops, sometimes to twenty below.

They spread across the prairie, the snowdrifts piled high.
And it all looks the same, the ground and snow filled sky.

The cattle drift with the storm trying to escape wind's icy
blast.
Single file, they keep on walking, until they find shelter at
last.

Their instinct prods them on, and they seem to know,
it is either to find shelter, or to perish in the snow.

They bunch in a brushy draw, or the leeward side of a hill.
And they stay right there, until the wind is still.

Those cattle have to be gathered, after the blizzard dies
down,
gathered and brought on back, back to the feeding
ground.

And there's just no way, you're going to keep warm,
when riding after cattle, that have drifted with the storm.

Your saddle time has increased, by ma nature's fickle,
quirk.
But you know that's all a part, of doing winter work.

We fed hay with a four-horse team when I was a kid. Then we started using a tractor, so I didn't feed with a team very long.

That way of doing it has pretty much been relegated to history and it has surely gotten easier now. I wouldn't want to do that anymore but I can look back on that time with a certain amount of nostalgia, of having been a part of that time.

Even though the day-to-day work was much more demanding, labor wise, it was a quieter, slower time, more laid back and less anxiety ridden. And, driving a team at twenty below, we were certainly more in communion with nature.

Four Horse Team

Four abreast, leaning into the collars,
tugs taut, muscles bunched, each doing its share.
Heaving sides, hooves scraping, flaring nostrils
breathing steam into the frozen air.

The thin link between team and driver,
ribbons of leather in strong callused hands.
Plied with the skill of a puppeteer,
that and voice commands.

"git up team, Sally move along,
Pete, you lazy old so and so."
A voice of authority and affection,
"steady now, and whoa."

Plodding through sparkling snow,
four abreast, lines wrapped slack.
Pulling steady and slow,
the driver pitching hay from a stack.

Four abreast, walking into the past,
the power of a bygone day.
Those big powerful gentle horses,
when work was done in a slower way.

Norman Licking feeding hay.

Rick Licking hooking up.

This hypothetical fellow may be a bit exaggerated, but any of us who have attended poetry gatherings have ran across someone like him.

I don't have a problem with someone walking the walk, and talking the talk, if they don't try to make folks believe they are something they aren't.

The Imposter

He swaggered in on a poetry session,
wearing a big hat and knee-high boots.
And started telling the folks there
that all his life, he'd been in cahoots,

with many cowboys and ranchers,
and had done his share of buckarooin'.
That, "just about most all his life,
it was mostly what he had been doin'."

He told about the big ranches he'd owned,
how he'd been in the rodeo game.
Cowboyin' now, according to him,
..."was gettin' down right tame."

He bragged about the good hand he'd been,
and the good cow-horses he'd rode.
Most of those in the audience knew,
he was shoveling them a big load.

All the cowboys there knew anyhow,
that this jasper was as phony as could be.
It strengthened what they already knew,
when he launched into his poetry.

Now, you can dress like a cowboy,
and you can recite a cowboy rhyme.
But try to make folks think you are one,
and you will get found out most every time.

Because there's something about a cowboy,
that goes beyond the swagger and the clothes.
It's in his looks, the way he walks and talks.
It's in his poetry. It's how he is... it shows.

DORSEY

As with many small towns, Wood Lake has outlived its usefulness. A once thriving town, it now has just a church, post office, café and elementary school.

There was a time when they figured they had to get rid of old unused buildings, no matter what kind of condition they were in. Fortunately they are beginning to rethink that, figuring these buildings are a connection to our past so maybe we should be preserving them.

They Tore the Hotel Down

They tore the hotel down,
where cattlemen would stay.
The old hotel is gone now,
but there was a long ago day,

When the little cow town lobby
saw cash and cattle collide.
And the weary drovers knew,
that tonight they'd sleep inside.

There were some mighty big deals,
and friendships made in that abode.
It housed so many travelers,
needing respite from the road.

Now a county metal shed sits
where the Lakeview Hotel was.
They tore that grand old hotel down,
they tore it down because

they're driven to get rid of the old,
so it can be replaced by the new.
I guess you could call that progress,
but it's like bidding a friend adieu.

* * * * * *

They tore the depot down,
they no longer were using it.
And for some of the town folk,
the depot naturally seemed to fit

in their scheme to get rid of the old,
when it is not in use no more.
That old abandoned depot, to them,
was just another useless eyesore.

* * * * * *

They tore the stockyards down,
tore them down for salvage.
Can't be having that old stuff there,
in this new modern advanced age.

The railroad stockyards east of town,
where they loaded cattle on the cars.
The cowboys bedded in the hotel.
after trailing herds from afar.

* * * * * *

I wonder do they know or care,
that the old was made to last.
And when they tear it down,
they are severing a link to our past.

Making the decision to quit ranching was probably the most difficult decision I have ever had to make. I think the reason for this is because ranching isn't just an occupation; it is a way of life.

I wrote this poem at that time. As you can see, a lot of anguish went into this poem.

Letting Go

I've made a deal to lease my place,
    and I've been selling the cattle.
I'll soon be moving on to town,
    but I'm not going to sell my saddle.

Nothing ever stays the same,
    though we may choose to think it might.
Been most all my life on this place,
    raised a family, tried to do right.
But sometimes the hanging on,
    just isn't worth the fight.

I've got these two young horses,
    they're coming along just fine.
Reckon I will take them with me,
    'cause now I sure oughta have the time

to put some schoolin' on those colts.
    Time was hard to find before.
I've trained some mighty good horses,
    but it has gotten to be a chore.

s'pose they'll get shorted some,
    now that my cows will be gone.
To make a good usin' horse
    you need cattle to work him on.

Maybe they'll hire me at the sale barn,
     so I can kind of keep in touch.
I could educate my horses,
     and I wouldn't cost them much.

I'm sure not married to those old cows,
     woulda been a rocky one if I had been.
They haven't treated me all that good,
     but then there's been the times when

the market has come up a bunch,
     and stayed there for awhile.
Gave me a chance to get ahead some,
     got me feelin' like wantin' to smile.

But, for the biggest share of it,
     it's been tough just holdin' my own.
Naw, I'm not gonna miss those cows,
     won't miss them at all when they're gone.
Reckon it's time to pull the plug,
     it's time to be movin' on.

I'll be leaving with integrity and pride,
     and my hard earned knowledge of cattle.
I'm hanging on to my spurs and chaps,
     and I'm not going to sell my saddle.

At the big cowboy poetry gathering at Arvada, Colorado they have theme sessions, with five different sessions running at one time.

One session I was in was "The aging Cowboy." Now I was very much familiar with the topic of that session. Anyway, attending a poetry gathering always inspires me to write some new poetry. When I got home I came up with this poem about an old cowboy

Going Back

"Head them into the wind son,
we gotta move them against the storm.
Don't have so very far to go,
then we'll be home where it's warm."

He's going back, in his mind,
but maybe that's not so bad.
I went to see him today,
and that's just about all he had.

He's going back in his mind,
to when he was ranching long ago.
And the things he used to do,
back then, before he had to go

to the county old folks home,
but he doesn't know he's there.
He's out on the land he loves,
Out where he's free, out where

the air is clean as nature made it,
where a man wants to take a big breath.
Where the air don't smell of medicine,
a lot of suffering, pain and... death.

I went to see him today,
and I was glad I had come.
From what I see, that old cowboy,
is much better off than some.

At least he's back out on his ranch,
working cattle, in his head.
Not in the county old folks home
laying weak and wore out, in a bed.

"Snub him up while I get on,
then I'll pull off the blind.
You fellers get on out of the way,
'cause this old boy's gonna unwind."

What will be the world of our grandchildren when they are as old as we are now? We will never know. We start to say "I remember when"… and then we stop, we "older" ones. We will never know what their world will be like, but some day they may read what our world was once like, and perhaps envy us.

Eleanor Seberger (Feb. 4, 1913 – Jan. 19, 2003)

This is a story about courage, faith and perseverance against over-whelming odds. This is about my father.

He Planted a Tree

He planted a tree, though he knew he would never sit in its shade.

I guess what I remember most about my dad was his struggle with severe asthma. I can remember dad sitting by the window, fighting for breath, punching his fist through the window screen in a futile attempt to get more air. An irrational act but restricted breathing causes irrationality.

I can just barely remember living in Colorado, where a doctor had sent dad for his health, which I don't think helped. The nation hadn't yet recovered from the devastating drought and depression. Dad worked long hard days with a team and pitchfork and whatever he could find to do, for near starvation wages. And he went house-to-house sharpening knives and scissors in an effort to keep his family sheltered and fed.

Dad's philosophy on life was a simple one that has not, or cannot, be improved upon. You did, without compromising your integrity, what you had to do to get by. Then, if you could, you gave it an extra measure to get ahead. You were honest in your dealings. You didn't take something that didn't belong to you and you didn't expect to get something you didn't earn. I think there could have possibly been a government or social agency where dad could have gotten financial aid, but I think if he had he wouldn't have felt right about it.

And I remember dad's determination to plant trees. Dad ranched on leased places, renting the home place twenty years before signing a contract to buy it. He planted trees as if he owned it. When dad died in 1968 he hadn't yet made a payment, but he had shelterbelts established that were beginning to offer protection to cattle.

Dad was also determined to plant seeds of resourcefulness and self-reliance in the minds of his children, and of other young people he temporarily raised. Dad's formal education was limited, as it was for many country children of that era. But he had a head for business and an unpretentious faith in his ability in what he did know. I remember dad trading for an outlaw horse that had been traded around the country and continually bucked off everyone who had owned him. Dad made a good horse of him and, as a youngster; I roped calves off that horse. Dad possessed a wealth of knowledge, taught by life, perseverance and hard work, knowledge that he strived to pass on to us.

Sometimes I get the feeling each generation has the opinion that they were born knowing more than the preceding one ever did. Each following generation, I come in contact with, makes me think that notion can only increase. There were times when I was impatient with dad because we didn't see eye to eye about something. But I can't think of a time I didn't figure I could learn from him, and I know there was never a time I didn't respect him. Not just because he was my father but also because my generation was ingrained with the attitude that you respected your elders.

I guess if dad had a vice that belied his gentle demeanor it was his penchant for practical jokes. Being a gullible child I was an easy mark for dad's pranks. I didn't have many years on me when dad decided I should break a renegade pony. I can't remember how many times that pony bucked me off that day as I rode along side dad, but it was a bunch. The pony was small and only my feelings were injured, especially when I began to realize that the dog probably had a bit of encouragement to nip the pony's heels and the boot toe in the flank wasn't entirely accidental.

I think dad really enjoyed the challenge of talking me back on each time.

Heaven

Lord, I would like my heaven to be
a little bit of each pretty place I have seen.
I don't want to walk on streets of gold,
but on grass that is always green.

I want to spend eternity
with a good cow horse to ride.
I don't know about playing the harp,
but I'll want my loved ones by my side.

I don't want to wear a robe of white,
or have a halo around my head.
Just my boots and Wranglers,
and old gray Stetson instead.

I don't want a set of wings,
to fly around heaven all day.
Just want to watch the birds fly,
and little calves at play.

I wonder what I'll do in heaven,
I can't set around and shirk.
I think I'd get mighty proddy,
if I didn't have some kind of work.

I don't want to work hard,
as I have always had to.
But I would be more contented,
if I had some little job to do.

I could wrangle heaven's remuda
and take my turn at ridin' drag.
Whatever it was that needed doin'
I'd do it Lord, and try not to lag.

I could gentle a scared, timid colt,
and maybe once in awhile rope a cow.
I'm not near the hand I used to be,
but Lord, you know I got the know how.

No one knows what heaven is like,
just what the good book has to say.
All who deserve it will find out,
on the judgement day.
I Think it will be a restful place,
for a tired old cowboy to stay.

"I have wondered at times about what the ten-commandments would have looked like if Moses had run them through the U.S. Congress."

Ronald Reagan

I can't understand the reluctance of congress to pass a law protecting our flag from abuse, especially now.

On June 14, 2007, my grandson Josiah was killed in Iraq and, whether we believe in the war over there or not, we should all be rallying in standing up for what the flag stands for. We should show our pride in this symbol of American freedom and way of life that is being threatened.

The Flag

It has flown over the beaches of Normandy,
and the sands of Afghanistan.
It has proudly waved over arenas
from Omaha to Cheyenne.

This symbol of American pride
has been cursed, trampled and torn,
in a display of insane hatred
by the radical ones, who scorn

the freedom we take for granted,
because we've known no other way.
But, when our nation gets trifled with
we have always been quick to pay

in blood and sweat, and lives.
We are willing to sacrifice,
to protect it from any foe.
We have always paid the price

of what it takes to keep it waving,
strong, and proud, to see.
Over all free Americans,
throughout this vast country.

About the Author

Most of a lifetime ranching and cowboying in north central Nebraska gives Willard Hollopeter the credentials to write cowboy poetry. Now retired from active ranching, he lives in the Small village of Wood Lake with his wife Mary.

The many years spent on the Sandhill ranch instilled a deep appreciation for that way of life and a respect for the land and those engaged in ranching.

Willard's poetry not only tells about the "Cowboy Way" but addresses conservation issues and he speaks what is on his mind about ranching changing too fast and about non-rancher types buying up vast acres of ranchland.

He tells of good horses and bad rides and of old worn out cowboys, and about wrecks that only a cowboy could survive. Much of his poetry is humorous, some is thought provoking and some is downright tear jerkin' sad.

Willard presents his poetry at gatherings and various functions. He also writes a newspaper column and has a weekly radio program.